When You Come Back
By Aaron Fields

Copyright © 2025 Aaron Fields. All rights reserved.

Published by The Write Perspective, LLC

All rights reserved. No part of this book shall be reproduced or transmitted in any form or by any means, electronic, mechanical, magnetic, photographic including photocopying, recording or by any information storage and retrieval system, without prior written permission of the publisher. No copyright liability is assumed with respect to the use of the information contained in this book. Even though every precaution has been taken in preparation for this book, the publisher/author assumes no responsibility for errors or omissions. Neither is any liability assumed for any damage that results from the use of the information in this book.

ISBN: 978-1953962-78-2

Theme: Separation anxiety, secure return, emotional rituals

Aman doesn't like goodbyes. His tummy flips when Papa picks up his bag.

"Do you have to go?" Aman asks. "I just got used to you being here."

Papa smiles. "I always come back. Just like always."

They put the hearts in their pockets. "Mine stays with you", says Papa.

Aman's face wobbles. A tear drops

Papa scoops him up. "It's okay to feel sad," he says. "I'll be back."

At school, Aman clutches his lion and watches Papa walk away.

"I miss him," Aman whispers. "My heart is squishy.

Miss Tasha kneels down. "It's hard to miss someone. I'm here too."

Aman draws a picture of Papa at work. "So he won't forget me."

At nap time, Aman sleeps with his lion and heart in his pocket.

The sun starts to go down. His tummy flips again but this time in a good way.

The door opens.

Aman runs. Papa lifts him high.

"You came back," Aman whispers.

"Just like always," Papa smiles

Notes for Adults

Separation can be deeply emotional for young children-----especially when they can't yet tell time or fully understand routines. Whether it's daycare, school, or a caregiver leaving for work, the stress of "goodbye" can show up as clinginess, tantrums or withdrawal.

The story was created to model:

- Predictable goodbye rituals
- Gentle emotional validation
- Secure attachment through return.

When children experience consistent reconnection, their nervous system learn that love can stretch across time. You don't have to promise you'll never leave--------just that you always come back.

You always come back.
Just like always.

www.ingramcontent.com/pod-product-compliance
Lightning Source LLC
Chambersburg PA
CBHW041433040426
42450CB00022B/3478